incredible journeys

Words by Anna Claybourne

Illustrations by Pauline Gregory

How OLD are you?
We're curious too, and we want to find out about YOU!
What's your NAME?
Where do you live on Planet Earth?

What activity do you do for fun?
What's the longest journey you've ever been on?
What's your favorite animal?
Who is your best friend?
If you could eat one food every day what would it be?
Where would you go for an adventure?

Why Go on a Journey?

Who did it first?

People sometimes try to be the first to do a particular journey, whether that's to the top of a mountain or across an ocean. **Thomas Stevens** was first to cycle around the world.

The Benz Patent-Motorwagen

How would you like to travel?

Whenever new forms of transportation are invented, people try to make incredible journeys using them. **Bertha Benz** drove 120 miles (194 km) in 1888 to whip up interest in the motorcar, which had recently been invented by her husband, Carl Benz.

What could possibly go wrong?

Lots of things – and they often remain a mystery. Japanese adventurer **Naomi Uemura** was the first person to reach the North Pole alone and to raft the Amazon solo. But he set off to climb the Alaskan mountain Denali in 1984, and never returned.

Can You Go Around the World in 80 Days?

In Jules Verne's 1872 novel, Phileas Fogg travels around the world in 80 days. In a time before cars or planes, this seemed an impossible feat. But someone soon attempted it for real!

Could Nellie make it?

In 1889, American news writer **Nellie Bly** set off to see if she really could go around the world in under 80 days. She did it in 72, setting a new world record!

Who did it first?

The first ever round-the-world trip was led by Portuguese explorer **Ferdinand Magellan**. The epic voyage began in 1519 and took 1,084 days. Sadly, Magellan died on the way. Of a crew of 240, only 30 made it all the way home.

Can You Swim Down the Amazon?

Slovenian swimmer **Martin Strel** swam the entire length of South America's Amazon River in 2007. He had to dodge deadly bull sharks and piranhas on the way.

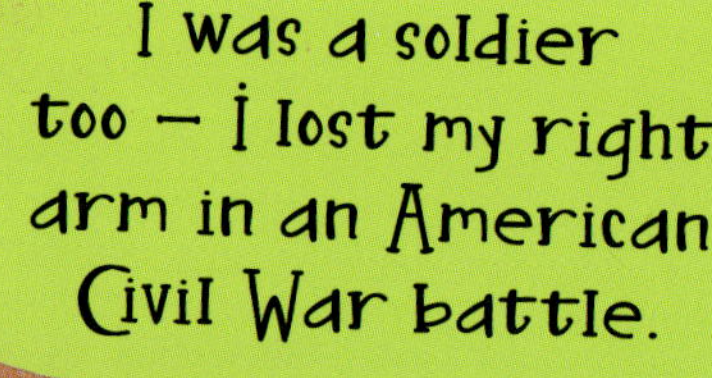

Where does this canyon go?

In 1869, American explorer and geologist **John Wesley Powell** led the first expedition by boat down the Colorado River through the remote Grand Canyon in Arizona. The journey made the canyon famous.

Who fought off a crocodile?

English explorer **Mary Kingsley** was famous for her journeys in Africa. In 1895, a crocodile climbed onto her canoe as she paddled up the Ogooué River in Gabon.

Who went over the falls in a barrel?

In 1901, 63-year-old retired teacher **Annie Edson Taylor** became the first person to go down the 167-foot-high Niagara Falls in a barrel (and survive!). The trip was NOT fun. Afterward, Annie said, "No one ought ever to do that again!"

Did You Know?

In 1993, Japanese yachtsman Kenichi Horie made the longest journey by pedal-powered boat – **4,600 miles (7,500 km)** from Hawaii to Japan.

The **deepest trip underground** was made by Pavel Demidov and his team in 2018, at the Verevnika Cave in Georgia.

You can go from Portugal to Singapore – **11,654 miles (18,755 km)** – by train. If there was a non-stop train on this route, it would take 12 days.

Portugal

Singapore

Only one more week of climbing to go!

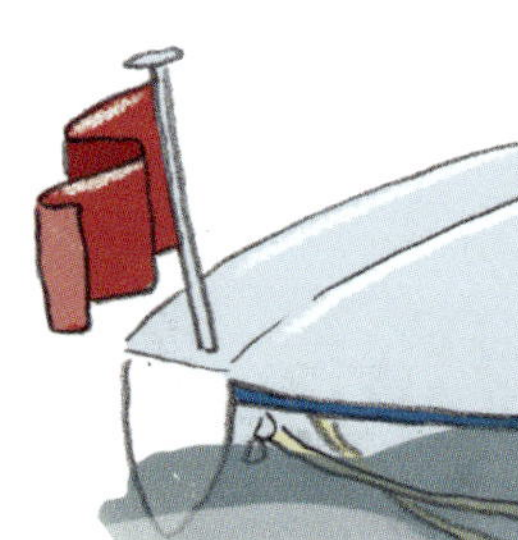

Are we nearly there?

The first time climbers made it up Canada's Mount Thor, the world's **tallest vertical cliff face**, it took them 33 days!

In 1964, Reg Spiers made the journey from the UK to Australia by **posting** himself inside a large box!

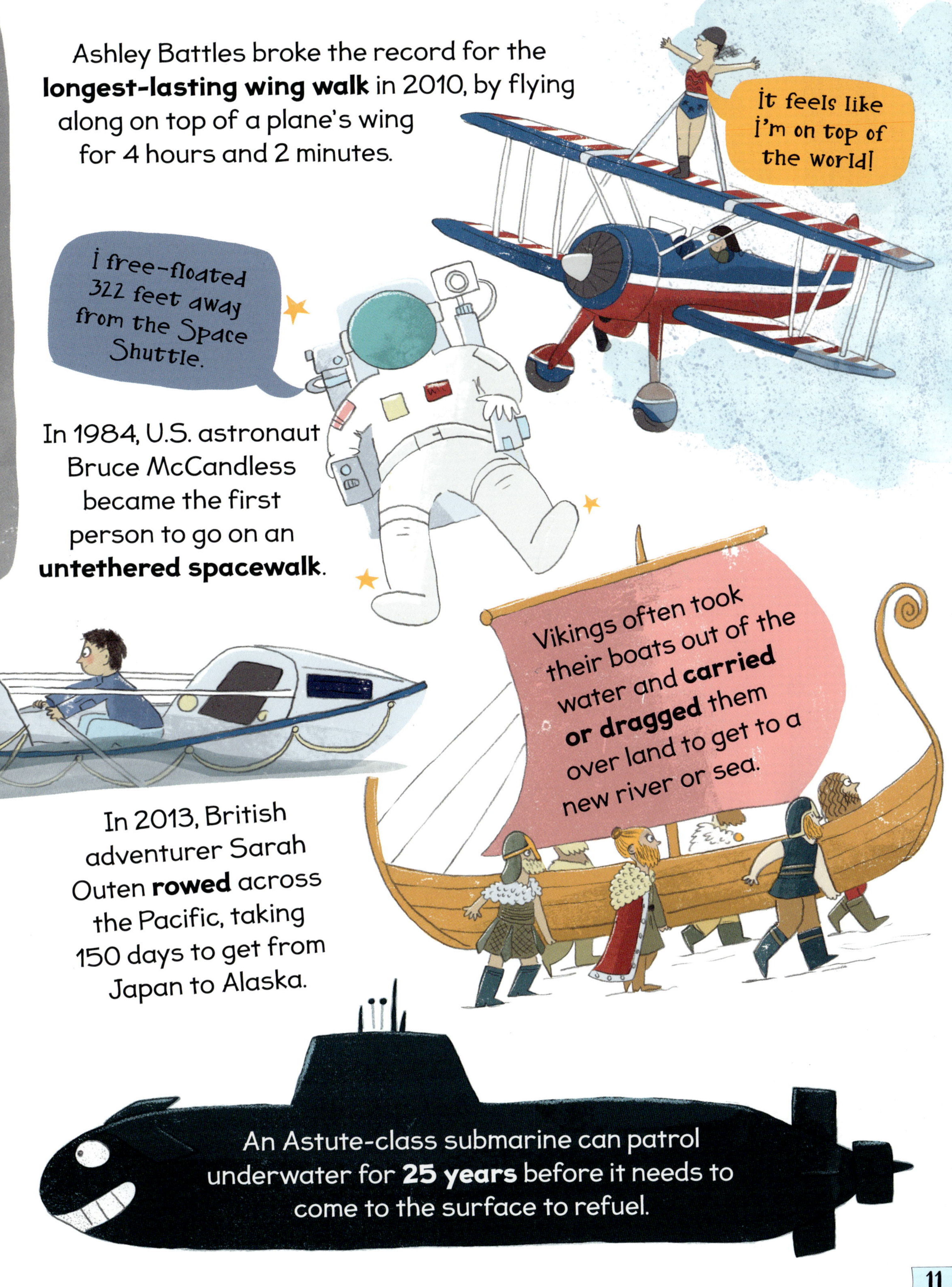

Ashley Battles broke the record for the **longest-lasting wing walk** in 2010, by flying along on top of a plane's wing for 4 hours and 2 minutes.

In 1984, U.S. astronaut Bruce McCandless became the first person to go on an **untethered spacewalk**.

In 2013, British adventurer Sarah Outen **rowed** across the Pacific, taking 150 days to get from Japan to Alaska.

An Astute-class submarine can patrol underwater for **25 years** before it needs to come to the surface to refuel.

Who Crossed the Pacific First?

Ferdinand Magellan and his crew were first to sail across the Pacific, on their around-the-world trip in 1521... or WERE they? Norwegian explorer **Thor Heyerdahl** wasn't so sure.

What did Thor think?

Heyerdahl believed ancient people could have sailed across the Pacific on simple rafts, long before Magellan's voyage. A trail of clues indicate that Pacific islanders and native Americans may have met up thousands of years ago.

Deep-sea canoe, used by ancient Polynesians

① Similar canoes in North America and Polynesia, made by sewing planks together

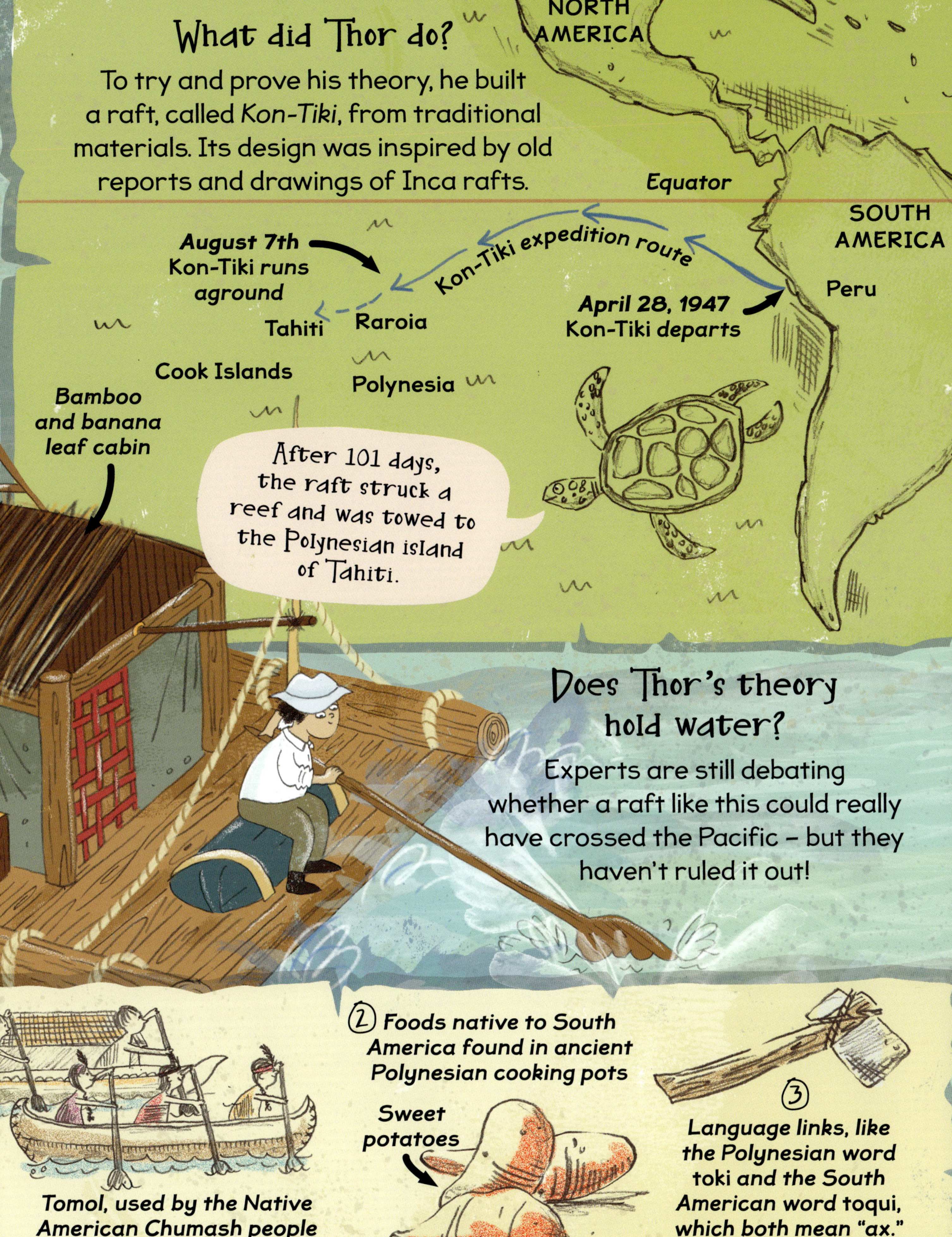

What did Thor do?

To try and prove his theory, he built a raft, called *Kon-Tiki*, from traditional materials. Its design was inspired by old reports and drawings of Inca rafts.

Does Thor's theory hold water?

Experts are still debating whether a raft like this could really have crossed the Pacific – but they haven't ruled it out!

Tomol, used by the Native American Chumash people

② Foods native to South America found in ancient Polynesian cooking pots

Sweet potatoes

③ Language links, like the Polynesian word toki and the South American word toqui, which both mean "ax."

Who Escaped from Antarctica?

In 1914, Irish adventurer **Ernest Shackleton** set off with a crew of men in his ship *Endurance*, to trek across Antarctica. But they soon faced a life-or-death struggle to survive.

Ernest Shackleton

① What went wrong?

As *Endurance* sailed toward Antarctica, it got trapped in sea ice.

② How did the ship sink?

The floating ice dragged *Endurance* off course. It was trapped for ten months, before being crushed by the pressure of the ice.

③ Who went to get help?

The men camped on the ice until it melted enough for them to sail to nearby Elephant Island. Then Shackleton and five others set off in a lifeboat to raise the alarm.

④

How did the crew survive?

They used the two remaining lifeboats, upturned, as shelter, and shared out their dwindling supplies as slowly as they could.

⑤ Did everyone get home?

Seventeen days and 808 miles (1,300 km) later, Shackleton reached South Georgia. He returned on a bigger boat for the stranded team.

⑥ What happened to the *Endurance*?

The wreck of *Endurance* was finally discovered on the seabed in 2022!

How Many?

19 The age of Zara Rutherford when she flew solo around the world, from 2021–2022.

Tiny Cessna 172

A truck on the ground refueled the plane twice a day.

Canadian explorer Aloha Wanderwell spent **5** years going around the world in a Ford Model T, an early model of car.

The longest continuous plane flight lasted for **64** days, from December 1958 to February 1959.

The world's shortest airline flight, between the islands of Westray and Papa Westray in Scotland takes just **1** minute.

Some freight trains in Canada can be **2.5** miles long!

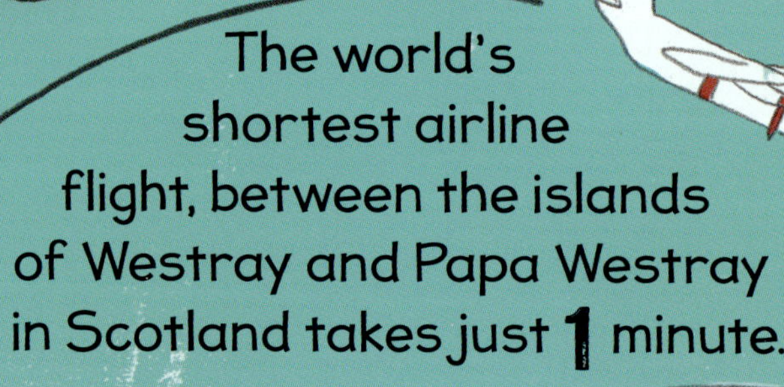

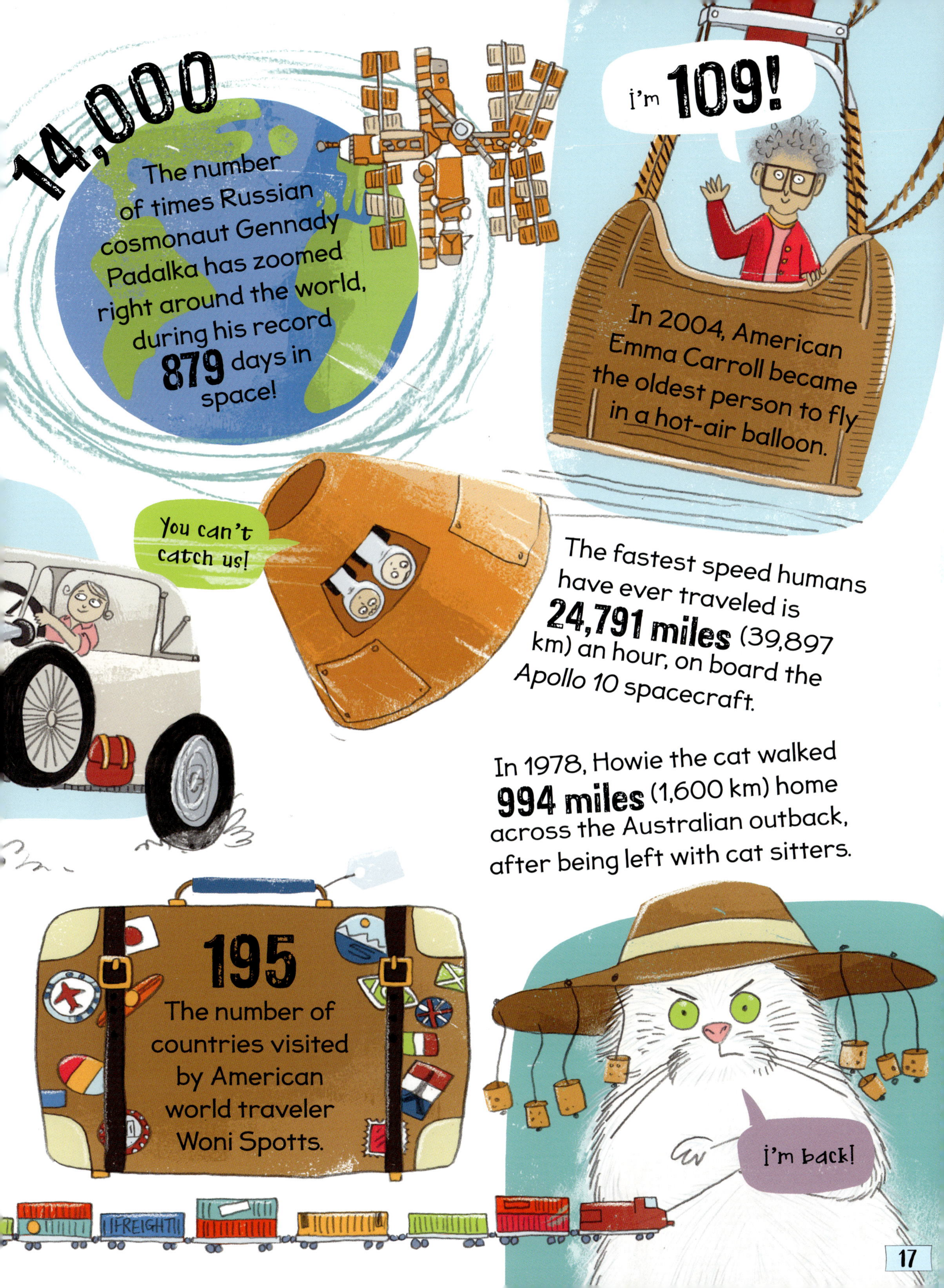

14,000

The number of times Russian cosmonaut Gennady Padalka has zoomed right around the world, during his record **879** days in space!

In 2004, American Emma Carroll became the oldest person to fly in a hot-air balloon.

The fastest speed humans have ever traveled is **24,791 miles** (39,897 km) an hour, on board the Apollo 10 spacecraft.

In 1978, Howie the cat walked **994 miles** (1,600 km) home across the Australian outback, after being left with cat sitters.

195

The number of countries visited by American world traveler Woni Spotts.

How High Can You Fly?

In 2005, Indian aviator **Vijaypat Singhania** flew into the record books by making the highest-ever hot-air balloon journey – 69,849 feet (21,290 m).

How high can you jump from?

A balloon filled with helium gas instead of hot air can go even higher. In 2014, engineer **Alan Eustace** soared to 135,889 feet (41,419 m) – then returned to the ground by parachute!

Can a balloon fly around the world?

Yes! **Bertrand Piccard** and **Brian Jones** did it in 2000 in their huge high-altitude balloon, Breitling Orbiter 3 – taking almost 20 days.

Who flew so high he passed out?

In 1862, **James Glaisher** fainted from lack of oxygen when he and **Henry Coxwell** flew to 28,871 feet (8,800 m) – higher than anyone had before. Coxwell's fingers froze, so he had to pull on a cord with his teeth to bring the balloon down safely.

Who was the first female balloonist?

French balloonist **Sophie Blanchard** was the first woman to fly solo in a balloon, in 1809. As well as flying across the Alps, she performed balloon displays, doing tricks and launching fireworks.

Why Did Darwin Travel the World?

In 1831, a ship named the *Beagle* set off from England on a five-year journey. **Charles Darwin**, a young naturalist, was on board to study rocks and wildlife.

① Darwin studied different species of finches in the Galápagos Islands.

NORTH AMERICA

What did Darwin discover?

Along the way, Darwin found many amazing species and fossils. They helped him understand evolution – the way living things change over time.

② Darwin noticed that the finches in different locations had small differences.

Galápagos

SOUTH AMERICA

Living things change and branch off from each other, like the branches of a tree!

③ Darwin realized that the finches had adapted (changed over time) in ways that helped them survive in their different environments.

Who ate the evidence?

The crew of the *Beagle*! In Patagonia, Darwin searched for a lesser rhea, a bird species locals had told him about. He finally found one on his dinner table after the *Beagle*'s crew had cooked it!

Darwin was amazed when he saw platypuses like me in Australia.

How Far Did Humboldt Go?

From 1799 to 1804, German naturalist and explorer **Alexander von Humboldt** journeyed over 5,965 miles (9,600 km) through parts of north, south, and central America and the Caribbean.

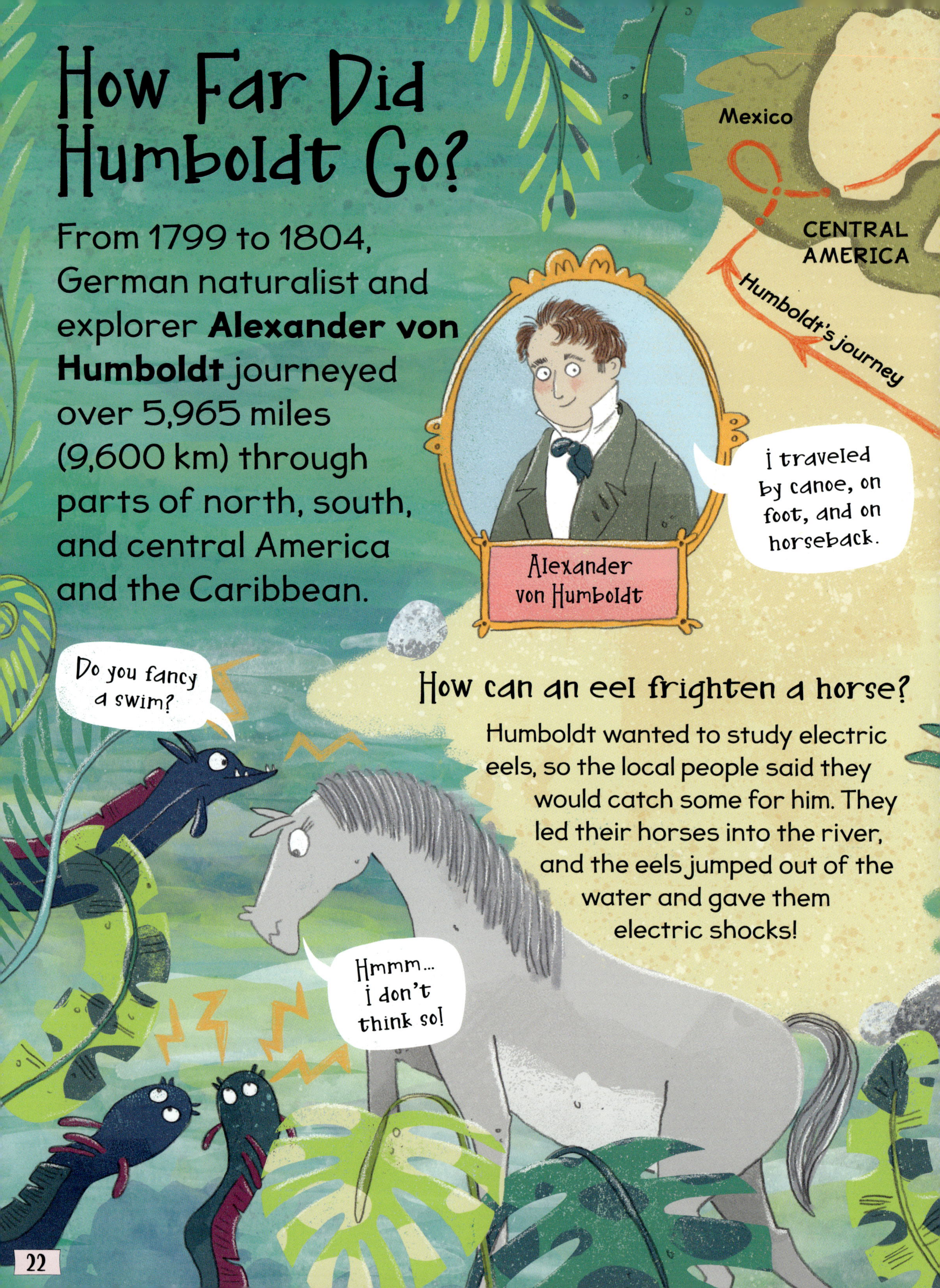

How can an eel frighten a horse?

Humboldt wanted to study electric eels, so the local people said they would catch some for him. They led their horses into the river, and the eels jumped out of the water and gave them electric shocks!

Who went in search of new caterpillars?

In 1699, Swiss scientist and artist **Maria Sibylla Merian** sailed all the way to Suriname to study its caterpillars. Until Merian recorded the process of metamorphosis, many people thought that butterflies came from mud!

Who walked through a flooded forest?

English adventurer **Ed Stafford** and his Peruvian guide **Gadiel Sanchez Rivera** WALKED across the Amazon rainforest, following the Amazon River. The journey of more than 3,728 miles (6,000 km) took 860 days.

Would You Rather?

Jump in the Orinoco River with an **electric eel**...

...or in the Amazon River with a **bull shark**?

Climb **Mount Everest**, or journey to the **bottom of the sea**?

Travel to Mars and stay for **two years**...

...or visit the Moon for a **single day**?

Parachute down from the freezing cold **stratosphere**...

...or trek to the freezing cold **South Pole**?

Get lost in a bone-dry, baking-hot **desert**, or a soggy, steamy **rainforest**?

Spend the night dangling halfway up a **cliff**, or in a deep, dark **cave**?

Zipline across the Grand Canyon or ride over the Niagara Falls in a **barrel**?

You can zoom along at over 100 miles (160 km) an hour on the fastest ziplines!

Go around the world on a **skateboard**, or in a **zorb ball**?

Fly **highest** or **fastest** in a hot-air balloon?

Travel with brave, crocodile-battling **Mary Kingsley** or bold, swashbuckling **Ernest Shackleton**?

Who Vanished into Thin Air?

After setting several flight records, famous aviator **Amelia Earhart** began a round-the-world journey in 1937. She was almost home when her plane vanished near Howland Island (her next stop) in the Pacific Ocean.

Earhart was never seen again. Some say she could have survived if she crash-landed on Nikumaroro Island.

Who nearly flew into a huge waterfall?

American pilot **Jimmie Angel** did! He was flying over the Venezuelan jungle in 1933 when he almost hit the world's tallest waterfall. Called *Kerepakupai Meru* by the local Pemon people, the falls became known to outsiders as Angel Falls.

Who hovered his way across the sea?

In 2019, French inventor **Franky Zapata** became the first person ever to cross the English Channel on a hoverboard.

The falls' indigenous name means "Water of the deepest place." They are 3,212 feet (979 m) high!

The Gossamer Albatross's top speed was only 18 miles (29 km) an hour!

Can you pedal a plane?

Yes! **Bryan Allen** flew across the English Channel in 1979. That alone wouldn't be remarkable, but Allen was a cyclist, and the plane, the *Gossamer Albatross*, was pedal-powered. Phew!

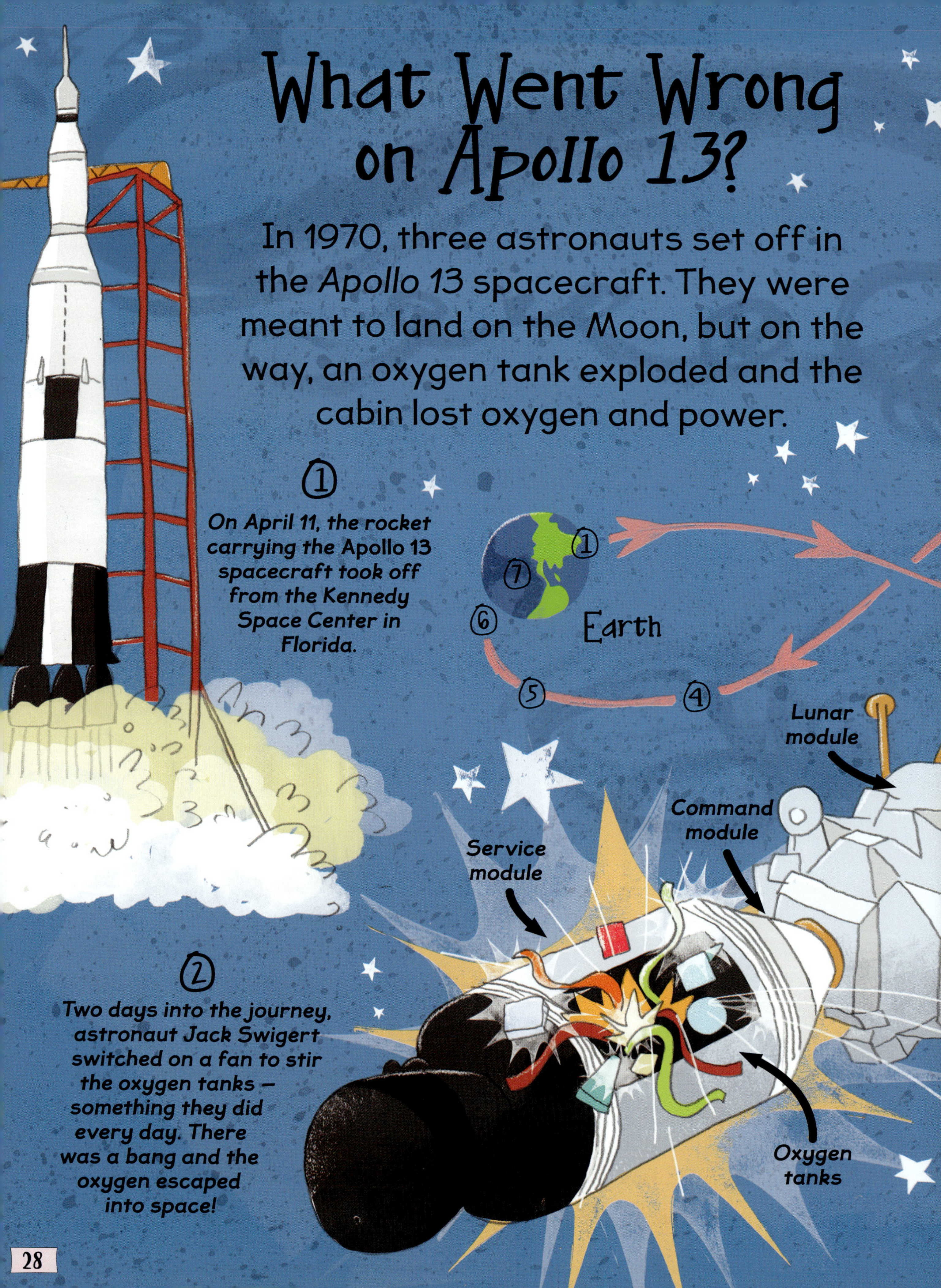

What Went Wrong on Apollo 13?

In 1970, three astronauts set off in the *Apollo 13* spacecraft. They were meant to land on the Moon, but on the way, an oxygen tank exploded and the cabin lost oxygen and power.

③ Did they make it to the Moon?

No – the crew had to abandon their main craft and escape into the tiny lunar module, designed for landing on the Moon's surface. Then, they looped around the Moon and headed home.

④ *The lunar module had enough oxygen, but the crew had to build makeshift equipment to clean the air they were breathing out.*

⑤ *On day six, as the crew approached Earth, they jettisoned the damaged service module.*

⑥ *The crew climbed back into the cone-shaped command module, and separated it from the lunar module to return to Earth.*

⑦ Did they get home?

Yes – the command module splashed down safely into the Pacific Ocean, and the crew was rescued.

A Compendium of Questions

Who got lost looking for a lost city?

In 1925, English adventurer Percy Fawcett went into the Amazon jungle to search for an ancient city, which he named the City of Z. He was never seen again...

What do you do if you see a mermaid?

If you're Henry Hudson, you record the sighting in your ship's log book! He wrote that the mermaid had pale skin, dark hair, and a porpoise-like tail.

We'll never know what Hudson really saw!

Who's been to space AND the bottom of the sea?

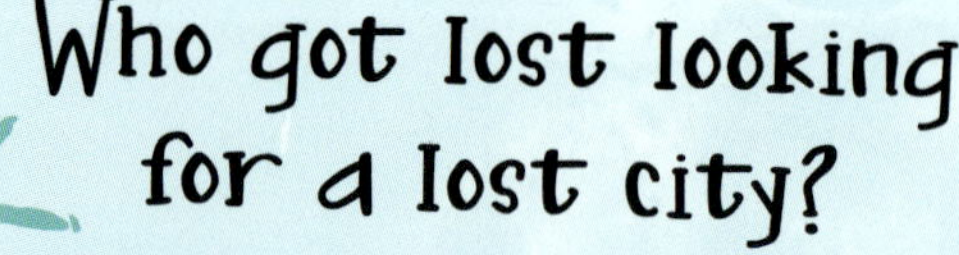

After a career as a NASA astronaut, Kathy Sullivan went on a dive to the bottom of Challenger Deep, the deepest part of the sea, in 2020.

How far can you go underground?

The Gotthard Base Tunnel in Switzerland burrows under the Alps, stretching 35 miles (57 km) between the towns of Erstfeld and Bodio.

Why was Pytheas puzzled?

Ancient Greek explorer Pytheas traveled north from Massalia (in today's France), perhaps as far as Iceland. He described how in midsummer, the Sun didn't go down for several days!

How long can a plane fly upside down?

American stunt pilot Joann Osterud flew her biplane upside-down for 4 hours and 38 minutes in 1991, covering a distance of 658 miles (1,059 km).

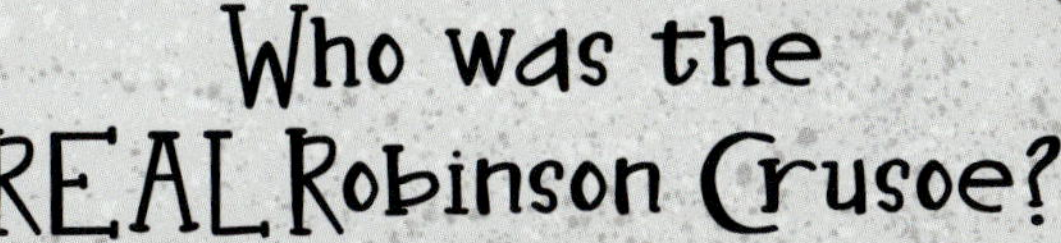

How far do we all travel every day?

About 29 million miles (47 million km) – as that's how fast the Earth is flying through space!

Who was the REAL Robinson Crusoe?

Daniel Defoe's 1719 book, which tells the tale of a castaway on a desert island, was based on a real person! Alexander Selkirk was a Scottish sailor who was marooned on an island in the Pacific.

Published in 2026 by Windmill Books,
an Imprint of Rosen Publishing
2544 Clinton St.
Buffalo, NY 14224

First published in 2023 by Miles Kelly Publishing Ltd
Copyright © Miles Kelly Publishing Ltd 2023

Publishing Director   Belinda Gallagher
Creative Director   Jo Cowan
Editorial Director   Rosie Neave
Senior Editor   Becky Miles
Design Manager   Simon Lee
Production   Elizabeth Collins
Reprographics   Stephan Davis

Cataloging-in-Publication Data
Names: Claybourne, Anna, author. | Gregory, Pauline, illustrator.
Title: Incredible journeys / by Anna Claybourne, illustrated by Pauline Gregory.
Description: Buffalo, NY : Windmill Books, 2026. | Series: Curious questions and answers about...
Identifiers: ISBN 9781538399019 (pbk.) | ISBN 9781538399026 (library bound) | ISBN 9781538399033 (ebook)
Subjects: LCSH: Voyages and travels--Juvenile literature. | Voyages around the world--Juvenile literature.
Classification: LCC G175.C539 2026 | DDC 910--dc23

Printed in the United States of America

CPSIA Compliance Information: Batch #CSWM26
For Further Information contact Rosen Publishing at 1-800-237-9932

Find us on